Why don't Astronauts BURP?

This edition published in 2021 by Arcturus Publishing Limited
26/27 Bickels Yard, 151–153 Bermondsey Street,
London SE1 3HA

Illustrator: Luke Séguin-Magee
Authors: Anne Rooney and William Potter
Editors: Susie Rae and Joe Harris
Designer: Rosie Bellwood

CH008347NT
Supplier: 10, Date 0621, Print run 11574

Printed in the UK

CONTENTS

GOODBYE, EARTH! 5

OUR WONKY WORLD 29

LUNAR LUNACY 53

PECULIAR PLANETS 79

THE OUTER LIMITS 107

ARE YOU READY FOR BLAST-OFF?

WOULD YOU LIKE TO TRAVEL TO ANOTHER PLANET, OR THE FARTHEST REACHES OF THE GALAXY? THEN BE PREPARED—THERE'S A LOT OF WEIRD, SCARY, AND DANGEROUS STUFF OUT THERE.

The universe is full of mindblowing wonders, huge, explosive forces, bizarre planets, weird science, and maybe even some other beings waiting to say hello! Get ready for a bumpy launch.

5...
4...
3...
2...
1...

LET'S GO!

GOODBYE, EARTH!

WHAT WAS THE FIRST THING HUMANS SENT INTO SPACE?

The first object to be put into space was a satellite called Sputnik, launched October 4, 1957 from the USSR. It was a shiny metal ball that looked like a spiky basketball, just 56 cm (22 in) across with four long radio antennae.

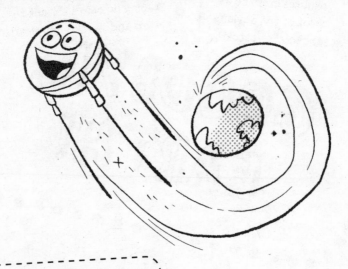

WHAT DID SPUTNIK DO?

Sputnik whizzed around in Earth orbit at 28,800 km/h (17,900 mph). It made 1,440 orbits, each taking just 96.2 minutes, before burning up re-entering Earth's atmosphere on January 4, 1958.

DID YOU KNOW?

For three weeks, Sputnik transmitted beeps that could be picked up even by amateur radio enthusiasts. It stopped transmitting when its batteries ran out.

WHO WAS THE FIRST HUMAN IN SPACE?

The first human being in space was Russian Yuri Gagarin on April 12, 1961. He spent just 89 minutes in space as pilot of the Soviet spacecraft Vostok 1.

WHAT DID GAGARIN'S MOTHER THINK?

Gagarin didn't tell his mother he was going because the mission was top secret. And he told his wife a later date for the flight (by which time he was home). Just in case, he left her a letter saying he didn't expect to return and she should remarry if he died.

WHO WAS THE FIRST WOMAN IN SPACE?

Russian cosmonaut Valentina Tereshkova became the first woman in space in 1963, with a three-day trip on Vostok 6. Tereshkova's mother found out when she saw the latest pictures from space on television. She knew her daughter had taken parachute training—but that's all!

IS THERE MUSIC IN SPACE?

The first music broadcast from another planet was a song by the US singer and rapper will.i.am of the Black Eyed Peas. NASA's Curiosity rover broadcast the song back to Earth, but didn't take speakers—so if there is any life on Mars, it didn't get to hear it.

DID YOU KNOW?

US astronauts Walter Schirra and Thomas P. Stafford were the first people to play musical instruments in space. They played "Jingle Bells" on an eight-note harmonica and bells while orbiting Earth on Gemini 6A in 1965. They pretended to be a UFO called Santa Claus.

CAN WE HEAR SOUNDS FROM OTHER PLANETS?

A rover due to land on Mars in 2021 is going to have microphones so it can send back to Earth the sounds of its own landing and travel across the surface of the planet. We'll be able to hear its wheels crunching over Martian stones.

HAS ANY SPACECRAFT LEFT THE SOLAR SYSTEM?

A robotic probe named Voyager 1 is the only spacecraft that has gone beyond the solar system—but Voyager 2 is on the way out, too. Both Voyagers were launched in 1977. Voyager 1 is now 21 billion km (13 billion miles) away. Voyager 1 is so far from the Sun that it takes 18 hours for sunlight to reach it. The spacecraft travels at 17 km (11 miles) per second.

WHAT WILL HAPPEN TO BOTH VOYAGERS?

The Voyagers' instruments will send back data to Earth until around 2030, when their power supplies will fail. The Voyagers will continue going at 48,280 km/h (30,000 mph) forever unless they are destroyed in a collision.

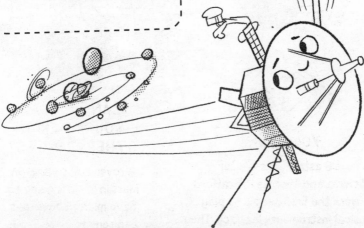

COULD THEY EVER LEAVE OUR GALAXY?

The Voyagers could never leave the galaxy, even in billions of years, because they're too slow to escape its gravity. It will be 40,000 years before either Voyager comes even slightly close to another star.

CAN YOU DRINK COFFEE IN SPACE?

In zero gravity, in a spaceship, liquids don't stay where they are. Coffee crawls out of its cup or bottle and floats around in the air.

WHY DON'T ASTRONAUTS BURP?

Without gravity, the gases and liquids in an astonaut's digestive system do not separate. So if an astronaut burped, liquid food would also come out of their mouth. Yuck!

CAN YOU EAT SALT IN SPACE?

Astronauts can only eat salt in liquid form, because tiny grains of salt might float away and clog air vents, damage machinery, or get stuck in an astronaut's eye!

HAVE METEORITES EVER HIT EARTH?

There are around 190 craters around the world that were created by fallen meteorites. The largest one is in South Africa——it measures more than 190 km (118 miles) in diameter and was created about 2 billion years ago.

WHY CAN'T YOU GO TO MARS IN A STRAIGHT LINE?

When spacecraft go to Mars, they loop around the Sun in a curved path. Earth and Mars orbit the Sun at different speeds. The best time to leave is calculated from the positions and speeds of both planets. Mars must be in the right place when the spacecraft's orbit intersects the orbit of Mars.

IS IT SAME FOR THE RETURN JOURNEY?

Astronauts couldn't just do their thing on Mars and then leave. They'd have to wait months for the planets to be in the right place for the return journey.

WHICH MARS ROVER HAS GONE THE FARTHEST?

Rovers travel over the surface of other planets and the Moon, but they don't go very far. The most adventurous rover is Opportunity on Mars. It covered 45 km (28 miles) between January 2004 and June 2018, at a stately pace of 180 m (590 ft) per hour.

HAVE WE TURNED SPACE INTO A DUMP?

Lots of old spacecraft are stuck in orbit around the Sun. When spacecraft are sent somewhere and fail to arrive, they don't just disappear—they end up going around the Sun. At least 34,000 bits of space junk are currently going around and around the Sun.

HOW LONG WILL THE JUNK STAY THERE?

The junk could keep going round the Sun for millions or billions of years.

IS THERE A CAR GOING AROUND THE SUN TOO?

Yes. In 2018, American businessman Elon Musk launched a red Tesla Roadster into space as a test load for the new Falcon Heavy rocket. It's "driven" by a dummy in a spacesuit. A plaque on the engine reads "Made on Earth by humans." The car will reach a maximum speed of 21,600 km/h (13.422 mph).

IS SPACE JUNK DANGEROUS?

Space junk is a real problem. Just as there's too much garbage on Earth, there's also too much of it in space. It could do real harm if it crashed into another satellite or a spacecraft, which is why all the space junk is tracked.

WHAT IS EARTH'S SPACE JUNK MADE OF?

Most space junk is bits and pieces of old satellites that no longer work, and discarded parts of rockets that are dropped when no longer needed. There are 20,000 pieces larger than a softball, 500,000 larger than a marble, and millions of smaller chunks.

CAN WE COLLECT CHUNKS OF ASTEROIDS?

The probe OSIRIS-REx, launched in 2016, reached the asteroid Bennu in 2018 to map its surface for two years. It will blow puffs of nitrogen gas at the asteroid to dislodge pieces. OSIRIS-REx will try to catch at least 60 g (2 oz) of material, then bring it back to Earth in 2023.

CAN WE MINE ASTEROIDS FOR PRECIOUS METALS?

A company based in California, USA, and Belgium intends to start mining asteroids for valuable metals and minerals. It's designing a spacecraft that will capture asteroids and drag them through space to a space station (not yet built) for processing.

WHY IS NASA WORKING ON AN "ICEMOLE?"

NASA will send an IceMole probe to look for life in the oceans of Saturn's moon Enceladus. The ocean beneath the frozen surface of this moon is one of the most likely places to find life beyond Earth.

WHAT MIGHT IT FIND?

It's not looking for large undersea creatures—maybe tiny microbes at the best. But who knows?

WHAT WOULD THE "ICEMOLE" DO?

The IceMole probe would melt through some of the ice and take samples. It's already been used to bore through ice in Antarctica.

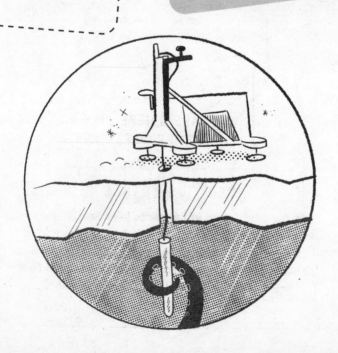

CAN YOU VOLUNTEER TO GO TO MARS?

When the Mars One Foundation asked for volunteers for a one-way trip, 200,000 people applied.

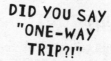

DID YOU SAY "ONE-WAY TRIP?!"

By far the hardest part of a trip to Mars is taking off for the return journey. Staying there avoids that problem.

WON'T IT GET LONELY?

You wouldn't necessarily be on your own for long. Every 26 months, Earth and Mars are in the right place for another spaceship to fly out, potentially taking more people.

ARE THERE ANY OTHER OPTIONS?

Another organization has plans to set up a colony on Mars, sending groups of people to live there permanently. One space scientist has suggested that just one person would go, or maybe a couple.

WHAT HAPPENS TO YOUR BODY IN SPACE?

Going into space isn't good for you. The heart shrinks without gravity, as it has less work to do pumping blood around the body. Bones weaken, as they don't have to work hard without gravity. Astronauts' muscles waste away unless they do lots of exercise—at least two hours a day.

DO YOU GROW TALLER IN SPACE?

Yes. People grow taller in space without gravity dragging them down. Identical twins Scott and Mark Kelly have been studied by NASA: Scott spent a year on the International Space Station (ISS) while Mark stayed on Earth and their health was compared. After a year in space, Scott Kelly grew 5 cm (2 in).

DID YOU KNOW?

If you cry in space, the tears don't fall—they clump together into a big ball that eventually floats away. Eyesight deteriorates, so astronauts who wear glasses often need stronger ones after a few months in space.

ARE THERE SPACE SPIDERS?

NASA sent two golden orb spiders to the International Space Station (ISS) for 45 days in 2011. They were called Gladys and Esmeralda and they became celebrities.

DID YOU KNOW?

An earlier attempt at the experiment was given up after eight days. The spiders eat fruit flies, and the astronauts released all the fruit flies into the spider habitat immediately. Soon, fruit-fly smear covered the glass, making it impossible to see what was happening inside the spider habitat.

CAN SPIDERS SPIN WEBS IN SPACE?

More than 130,000 students signed up to follow the investigation into how well Gladys and Esmeralda could spin webs in microgravity. (Pretty well, as it turned out.)

DOES TIME GO AT A DIFFERENT SPEED IN SPACE?

Yes. Astronauts age more slowly than people stuck on Earth, but only very slightly. Time goes more slowly on the International Space Station (ISS) than on Earth. An astronaut on the ISS gains just one hundredth of a second a year.

WHO HAS FLOWN THE FASTEST IN SPACE?

No human has ever flown faster than the crew of Apollo 10. On the way back from orbiting the Moon in 1969, Apollo 10 reached 39,897 km/h (24,791 mph)—the fastest speed ever achieved by a vehicle carrying a crew.

WHICH SPACECRAFT HAS FLOWN THE FASTEST IN SPACE?

The uncrewed robotic spacecraft Juno reached 266,000 km/h (165,000 mph) as it was pulled toward Jupiter by the planet's gravity in 2014. But the Parker Solar Probe, heading for the Sun, will have a top speed of 692,000 km/h (430,000 mph).

COULD EARTH SPACECRAFT HARM ALIENS?

Every spacecraft carries some microbes from Earth into space. These could contaminate a planet or moon that might have life of its own, possibly causing harm or changing the course of evolution.

HOW CAN WE MAKE SPACECRAFT SAFE FROM BUGS?

Under an international agreement, all spacecraft are cleaned thoroughly to destroy any microbes. The target is to take no more than 300,000 microbes on any spacecraft.

DID YOU KNOW?

The Juno spacecraft, sent to explore Jupiter and its moons, plunged into the huge gas giant at the end of its mission so it couldn't crash into one of the moons that might have some form of life.

IS THERE A PLACE ON EARTH FOR ALIENS TO LAND?

A town in Wyoming, USA, had a spaceport for aliens from Jupiter. For around 20 years from 1994, the town of Green River had the only spaceport set up to welcome refugees from Jupiter.

WHY JUPITER?

That year, NASA reported that Jupiter was in danger of being struck by broken chunks of comet. The residents of Green River worried about the creatures living on Jupiter (if there were any) and decided to welcome them.

WHAT WILL ALIENS FIND THERE?

It was the only official intergalactic space port in the world, but it only had a windsock and a welcoming sign.

WHAT ANIMALS HAVE BEEN INTO SPACE?

Lots of different animals have been into space, including spiders, chicken embryos (in their eggs), newts, jellyfish, bees, and even Mexican jumping beans (there's a worm inside the bean). The first living things sent into space were tiny fruit flies in 1947. They returned safely. A mouse survived going up into space in 1950, but the rocket fell apart coming back and it died.

WHAT ABOUT DOGS?

The most famous animal in space was a Russian stray dog, Laika, in 1957. Sadly, she died on the flight. Also, two Russian dogs, Veterok and Ugolyok, spent 22 days on Kosmos 110 in 1966, setting a record.

HAVE ANY MONKEYS BEEN TO SPACE?

The first monkey to reach space was Albert II in 1949, but he died on the return journey. In 1959, two monkeys called Able and Miss Baker survived a 16-minute flight and returned safely.

HOW DO JELLYFISH COPE WITH BEING IN SPACE?

In the 1990s, astronauts bred more than 60,000 jellyfish on the space shuttle Columbia to investigate how they use gravity—and found out they can't cope.

WHAT HAPPENS TO THEM?

Jellyfish have a special organ to tell them which way up they are. Tiny crystals roll around in a pocket lined with little hairs. The way that the hairs are disturbed tells the jellyfish which way is up and which way is down. In the microgravity of space, there is no up or down, so the jellyfish never learn to "read" the movement of the hairs.

WHAT HAPPENS WHEN THE JELLYFISH RETURN TO EARTH?

When they come back to Earth, their bodies can't understand gravity and they remain forever confused.

WHICH SPACECRAFT SENT THE FIRST DATA FROM ANOTHER PLANET?

In 1970, the Soviet spacecraft Venera 7 arrived at the planet Venus, but it didn't get a soft landing. Its parachute ripped and collapsed on the way through the acidic atmosphere, and Venera slammed into the scorching surface of Venus. It sent back data on its way down, but it then crashed and rolled over so that its antenna was not pointing toward Earth.

WAS VENERA 7 DESTROYED?

It seemed to go silent, but a week later scientists reviewing the tapes discovered that it continued sending a weak signal for 23 minutes, gaining its place in the record books.

CAN ROBOTS HELP US EXPLORE OTHER PLANETS?

NASA's Valkyrie robot will help build on Mars. Valkyrie (or R5) is a humanlike robot, 1.9 m (6 ft 2 in) tall and weighing a hefty 125 kg (275 lb). It can walk, see, use its hands—and put up with terrible working conditions.

WHAT WILL VALKYRIE DO?

It will work alongside astronauts on Mars, building shelters, mining for resources, and helping out with any problems.

WHAT WAS THE FIRST HUMANOID ROBOT IN SPACE?

The first humanoid robot in space was Robonaut 2.0, used on the International Space Station from 2012. Robonaut originally had no legs, but has been given two "climbing manipulators."

WHAT WAS THE FIRST SPACE STATION?

The first space station was Mir, started in 1986. Intended to last five years, it survived 15 years, until 2001. Mir was still going after the country that built it had stopped existing—the USSR broke up in 1991, but Mir lasted another 10 years.

WHAT HAPPENED TO MIR?

Mir orbited the Earth 86,000 times before breaking up and falling into the sea and over Canada, Australia, and South America.

WAS THERE A US SPACE STATION?

The United States' only space station, Skylab, was always called an "orbital workshop." Skylab lasted five years, from 1974 to 1979, and had crew for only 171 days of that time. When it fell to Earth, a US newspaper offered a $10,000 prize for finding a piece of it. A 17-year-old Australian claimed it after chunks of the falling Skylab hit his house.

WHO HAS STAYED IN SPACE THE LONGEST?

Cosmonaut Valeri Polyakov holds the record for the longest stay in space. He spent nearly 438 days on the space station Mir in a single visit in 1994-1995. That's more than a year and two months.

WHO HAS SPENT THE MOST TIME OUTSIDE A SPACECRAFT?

Russian Anatoly Solovyev has spent the longest time outside a spacecraft in space. He's made 16 space walks, adding up to more than 82 hours and 22 minutes.

WHO HAS SPENT THE MOST TIME IN SPACE?

The person who has spent most time in space all together is cosmonaut Gennady Padalka, who has spent a total of 878 days in space over five missions on the ISS and the Russian space station Mir.

OUR WONKY WORLD

DOES EARTH HAVE CRATERS LIKE THE MOON?

Earth is the only rocky planet in the solar system with few craters. Mercury, Mars, and Venus are pitted with huge craters. So is the Moon, but Earth has very few.

WHY DON'T WE SEE LOTS OF CRATERS ON EARTH?

It's not because the Earth isn't hit by things, but because its surface "heals." Wind, rain, moving ice, flowing floods, rivers, and the seas all wear away the surface of the Earth, so craters are soon smoothed out. But some are still visible.

WHERE CAN YOU FIND A REALLY BIG EARTH CRATER?

The Vredefort Crater in South Africa was 380 km (236 miles) across when first created by a massive space rock 2 billion years ago. It's about a third the size of Germany.

WHAT CAUSES THE NORTHERN LIGHTS?

The Northern and Southern lights are spectacular displays of swirling, changing shades of green, blue, yellow, red, and violet in the sky. They're made by tiny charged particles streaming from the Sun and colliding with the gases of Earth's atmosphere.

CAN YOU SEE THE NORTHERN LIGHTS FROM SPACE?

They're only seen near the North and South poles because Earth's magnetic field pulls the particles toward Earth at the poles. The patterns show up at both poles at the same time and are usually mirror images of each other. And, yes, they can even be seen from space!

DID YOU KNOW?

Sometimes it's dark all day at the North and South poles. Each pole is turned toward the Sun for part of the year and away from the Sun for part of the year. In December, the North Pole gets no light at all and, in June, the South Pole gets no light.

DO ROCKS FROM SPACE HIT EARTH?

Rocks from space hit Earth all the time. Meteors bombard Earth constantly but, as they whizz through the atmosphere, most get so hot that they burn up completely.

ARE METEORS THE SAME AS SHOOTING STARS?

If they are big enough, we see these burning meteors in the atmosphere as shooting stars.

WHAT ARE METEORITES?

The bits of space rock that make it to Earth's surface are called meteorites. They're not all big lumps of rock or metal. Most are micrometeorites, so tiny you need a magnifying glass or microscope to see them.

DID YOU KNOW?

There are micrometeorites in your home. They don't fall fast enough to burn up in Earth's atmosphere and are small enough to go everywhere.

WHAT IF A REALLY BIG ROCK FROM SPACE HIT EARTH?

Space rocks can be deadly. An asteroid that smashed into the Earth about 65 million years ago changed the conditions on the planet so much that many kinds of plants and animals died out, including most dinosaurs.

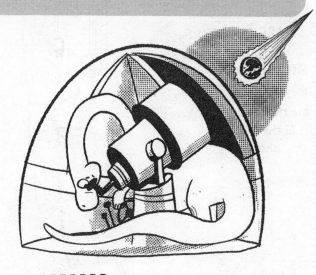

HOW BIG WAS THE ASTEROID THAT HELPED CAUSE THE END OF THE DINOSAURS?

The crater made by the huge space rock was found in the Gulf of Mexico in 1978. The asteroid would have been 15 km (9.3 miles) across.

DID YOU KNOW?

A substance called iridium, which is rare on Earth but common in asteroids, is found in rock layers around the world from 65 million years ago. This suggests tiny pieces of the asteroid spread around the globe.

HAVE EARTH DAYS ALWAYS BEEN 24 HOURS?

No. Days were shorter in the time of the dinosaurs. When Earth first formed, it whizzed round on its axis, four or five times as fast as it does now, and days were just 5-6 hours long, or maybe even shorter.

WHY DID EARTH DAYS BECOME LONGER?

Once the Moon formed, the effort of dragging it around slowed the Earth's rotation and the days got longer.

ARE DAYS STILL GETTING LONGER?

Yes. The Earth is still slowing down. In 100 years, a day will be two thousandths (0.02) of a second longer than it is now. That means that in 50,000 years, a day will be a whole second longer. It doesn't sound like much—but over millions of years, it really adds up!

WHY IS THE EARTH LIKE AN ONION?

Like an onion, the Earth is made up of layers. We live on the crust—the rocks and water that make up the land and seabed. The crust occupies just one hundredth of the volume of the planet. It's about 30 km (18 miles) thick on land and 5 km (3 miles) thick under the oceans.

WHAT'S UNDER EARTH CRUST?

Beneath the crust, a thick layer of very hot, molten, semi-liquid rock called magma oozes slowly around the planet. Magma makes up about 84 percent of the planet. Right in the middle, Earth has a super-hot iron core. The outer part of it is molten, and the inner part is a solid ball.

WHAT ARE TECTONIC PLATES?

Earth's crust is divided into chunks called tectonic plates. The plates are carried very slowly around the Earth as they float on top of magma. Where the edges of plates meet, volcanoes and earthquakes are common.

IS THE EARTH ROUND?

Not exactly. The Earth has a fat middle—it's more like a ball that has been squashed from top and bottom, making the middle fatter than it should be and the poles a bit flatter.

SO, WHAT SHAPE IS THE EARTH?

This shape is called an "oblate spheroid," and the chubby piece is called the "equatorial bulge." As the Earth spins on its axis, the forces acting on it push more matter toward the Equator.

HOW BIG IS EARTH'S "BULGE?"

If we measure the Earth pole-to-pole and around the Equator, the diameter at the Equator is 42.7 km (26.5 miles) larger than the diameter at the poles.

DOES THE EARTH HAVE MORE THAN ONE MOON?

Earth has a micro-"moon"—but it only counts as an asteroid. It's called 2016 HO3, which is not a very exciting name for a cosmic companion. It shares Earth's orbit around the Sun and seems to loop around Earth all the time, too.

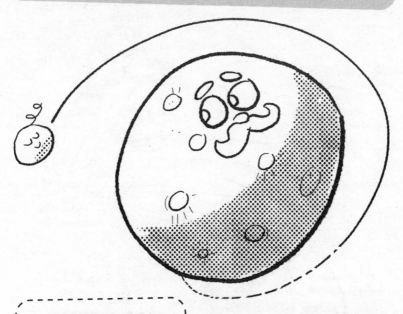

WHERE IS IT?

Earth's micro-"moon" is about 38 times as far away as the Moon and is only 40-110 m (130-360 ft) across. HO3 is called a "quasi-satellite." It's not close enough or permanent enough to count as a real moon.

HOW LONG HAS IT BEEN THERE?

HO3 has been hanging around Earth for about 100 years, and it will stay with us for several more centuries before drifting away.

HOW FAST IS THE EARTH SPINNING?

You're moving at over half a million miles an hour. If you stood still at the Equator, Earth's rotation on its axis would mean you'd be moving at 1,600 km/h (1,000 mph). You don't notice it because everything else is moving, too.

HOW FAST IS THE EARTH MOVING AROUND THE SUN?

The Earth is moving round the Sun at 108,000 km/h (67,000 mph). It goes around the Sun every 365.25 days, making a year. (We collect up the quarter days and have an extra day in a leap year, every four years.)

HOW FAST IS THE SOLAR SYSTEM MOVING?

The whole solar system goes around the middle of our galaxy, the Milky Way, but that huge circle takes 230 million years to complete. The last time we were where we are now, the dinosaurs were just getting started!

HOW DID LIFE ON EARTH BEGIN?

Some scientists think life on Earth came from space. They're not suggesting huge lions, whales, or dinosaurs came from space, but tiny microbes, carried on comets or asteroids or just floating around in space.

DID LIFE ON EARTH EVOLVE FROM ALIENS?

Microbes from outer space could have landed on Earth, and Earth could have had just the right conditions for them to flourish—meaning life on Earth could have evolved from aliens! This theory could explain life in many different star systems. So far, though, we haven't found any microbes on asteroids or comets.

CAN ANY CREATURE SURVIVE IN SPACE WITHOUT A SPACESUIT?

Water bears, or tardigrades, are tiny, tough creatures a fraction of an inch long. They've survived being outside in outer space, where they're freezing cold, bombarded with radiation, and have no oxygen.

WHY DOES EARTH HAVE SEASONS?

We have seasons because the Earth is wonky. The northern half of the world is tilted 23.5 degrees toward the Sun for part of the year, and the southern half for the opposite part of the year.

HOW DO SEASONS AFFECT PLANTS?

With longer days and more heat and light from the Sun, plants grow better in the summer.

WHAT ARE SOLSTICES AND EQUINOXES?

The solstices are the times of year when one end of the world has its shortest day and the other has its longest day. The equinoxes fall halfway between the solstices; days and nights are equal lengths at the equinox.

WHY IS THE SKY BLUE?

Light from the Sun is white, but white light is made up of a whole rainbow of shades. When the white light comes through Earth's atmosphere, the blue light is scattered more than the red, yellow, or green light—so the sky looks blue.

WHY DOES THE SKY LOOK DIFFERENT AT SUNSET?

At sunset, the light from the Sun has passed through a lot of atmosphere by the time it reaches us and a lot of the blue light has been scattered away. We see yellow light or, if there is dust in the atmosphere, red and orange. So sunsets come from a "dirty" sky.

WHY IS EARTH COLDER AT THE POLES?

The rays that bring light and heat from the Sun strike Earth from right above the Equator, but from a lower angle elsewhere in the sky. At the poles, the same amount of sunlight is spread out over a greater area of land, so it has less heating effect.

HOW HOT IS THE EARTH?

Earth is heated from the inside. The middle of the Earth is really hot—about 6,000 °C (10,800 °F). The heat comes from the decay of radioactive material and the leftover heat from the time Earth formed, 4,600 billion years ago.

WHY IS THE EARTH NOT HOT ON THE SURFACE?

Earth's own heat has the most impact underground. At the surface, it accounts for only 0.03 percent of Earth's heat energy, with all the rest coming from the Sun.

WHY DOESN'T ALL THE EARTH FREEZE AT NIGHT?

The Earth's atmosphere makes a good blanket, trapping heat close to the surface. Without it, a lot of heat would escape at night and heat would beat down on us during the day (and we'd have nothing to breathe!)

WAS EARTH ONCE A SNOWBALL?

Maybe more than once! Extreme climate change has happened several times in Earth's history. About 700-600 million years ago, the Earth's surface was covered with ice and the average temperature was just -50°C (-58°F). Early life forms skulked deep in the oceans to keep going.

HOW DID THE EARTH WARM UP?

Once the surface was all white, it reflected back all the heat from the Sun, so it couldn't warm up again. It could have gone on forever, but the Earth's volcanoes came to the rescue. They poured out carbon dioxide that trapped heat and slowly warmed the Earth again.

DID YOU KNOW?

When a volcano erupts, scorching hot, molten rock from inside the Earth pours out through a gap in the surface. While it's inside, it's called magma, but once it's outside it's called lava.

HOW WOULD ALIENS KNOW EARTH WAS INHABITED?

If aliens got close enough, they might notice radio waves that have leaked out into space. All the satellites and space junk orbiting the Earth and the Sun are a clue too. If they got close enough, aliens could see lights and pollution, and could spot chemicals in our atmosphere that are a sign of life.

WHAT WOULD HAPPEN IF ALIENS VISITED MARS OR THE MOON?

If they investigated the Moon or Mars, aliens might spot our abandoned spacecraft.

WHAT IF ALIENS PASSED HUNDREDS OF LIGHT YEARS AWAY?

If they are more than 100 light years away, none of our radio signals will have reached them, but a chemical map of Earth could show how we have moved some substances around and deposited them in odd places.

IS THE EARTH A BIG MAGNET?

At the Earth's core, liquid iron is moving around solid iron. This turns the Earth into a magnet, with one magnetic pole near the Geographic North Pole and one near the Geographic South Pole. The magnetic field extends out into space and affects the solar wind (particles streaming from the Sun).

WILL WE ALWAYS HAVE A NORTH AND SOUTH POLE?

Every now and then, the Earth's poles switch around, so the north magnetic pole ends up near the South Pole.

WHEN WILL THE NEXT SWITCH HAPPEN?

The last switch was 780,000 years ago, and many scientists think the Earth is gearing up for another switch. But it takes a long time to happen—more like 1,000 years!

HAVE ANY LARGE ASTEROIDS HIT EARTH IN RECENT HISTORY?

A massive explosion in the air over Russia, called the Tunguska Event, was probably caused by a huge asteroid. It flattened 2,000 square km (770 square miles) of forest—about 80 million trees—on June 30, 1908. Luckily, no one lived underneath.

DID THE ASTEROID CAUSE A FIRE?

It made a fireball 50-100 m (165-330 ft) across. Scientists think it was caused by an asteroid exploding as it passed through Earth's atmosphere.

HOW OFTEN DO THESE HUGE ASTEROIDS HIT EARTH?

Asteroids this size might hit the Earth every 100-200 years.

WHICH IS THE NEAREST PLANET TO EARTH?

Earth's nearest planet is Mars—usually. Sometimes it's Venus. They swap around!

HOW CAN PLANETS SWAP POSITION?

Mars, Venus, and Earth all orbit around the Sun at different speeds, which means Mars and Earth are sometimes on opposite sides of the Sun. Venus is on a smaller orbit than Mars because it's closer to the Sun.

ARE AMERICA AND EUROPE DRIFTING APART?

Yes! The Atlantic Ocean is growing wider at the rate of about 2.5 cm (1 in) a year as a new seabed wells up from the middle of the ocean. A rift in the Earth's surface runs right through the middle of the island of Iceland, so Iceland will slowly be split in half.

WHAT ABOUT THE OTHER SIDE OF THE WORLD?

On the other side of the world, the Pacific Ocean is getting narrower. One day in the distant future, America and Asia will be pushed together and the Pacific Ocean will close up—but not for hundreds of millions of years.

WAS INDIA ONCE AN ISLAND?

200 million years ago, most of the land on Earth was bunched up into a single supercontinent called Pangaea. India was an island that slowly drifted north. Its collision with Asia created Earth's tallest mountain range, the Himalayas.

HOW DOES "SPACE WEATHER" AFFECT EARTH?

Space weather can affect GPS and communications satellites so they don't work properly. It can disrupt the electric power grid that brings electricity to your home and school. It can produce drag that makes satellites drift off their orbits slightly, too.

IS THERE WEATHER IN SPACE?

You don't just have to worry about rain on Earth—space weather affects the planet, too. The "weather" in space is produced by bursts of energy of different kinds and particles from the Sun.

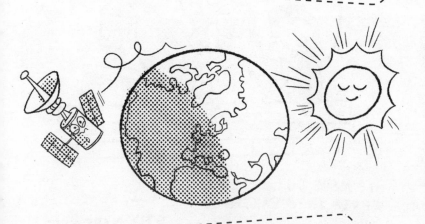

DOES "SPACE WEATHER" AFFECT EARTH WEATHER?

All of Earth's weather system depends on the Sun, so when the Sun does something odd, we can expect something odd down here.

IS MARS GETTING CLOSER TO EARTH?

In 2003, Mars came within 56 million km (35 million miles) of Earth—the closest it's been in 60,000 years. It will get even closer in 2287 and even closer still in 2729.

IS MARS GOING TO CRASH INTO EARTH?

No, Mars isn't on a slow collision course. The planets do a complicated dance around the Sun, with their orbits changing very slightly over patterns of thousands and even millions of years.

WILL MARS KEEP GETTING CLOSER TO EARTH?

No. After 25,000 years, Mars will start to move a bit further away again.

HOW HIGH DOES EARTH'S ATMOSPHERE REACH?

Earth's atmosphere stretches 10,000 km (6,214 miles) into space, but it's very thin at the top. The gases in the exosphere (outer layer) are so thin that they don't work like an atmosphere, but are still held by Earth's gravity. The piece we live in is called the troposphere.

WAS EARTH'S ATMOSPHERE ALWAYS LIKE IT IS NOW?

We breathe the Earth's third attempt at an atmosphere. The first was mostly hydrogen-based gases. Then, lots of volcanoes poured different gases into the atmosphere, so it became mostly nitrogen, carbon dioxide, and water. Finally, tiny bacteria producing oxygen changed the atmosphere again. Now our atmosphere is about a fifth oxygen.

IS THERE LIFE ON OTHER PLANETS IN THE SOLAR SYSTEM?

Earth is the only planet to have life. None of the other planets or moons in the solar system are likely to have life, except, just possibly, tiny microbes.

HOW MANY DIFFERENT SPECIES ARE THERE ON EARTH?

Earth has about 8.7 million different species. Over 99 percent of all species that have ever lived have died out.

HOW LONG DID IT TAKE FOR LIFE TO BEGIN ON EARTH?

It took just 250-500 million years before chemicals got together and made the earliest life forms, but another 3.5 billion years before large life forms started to grow in Earth's oceans. Humans appeared only 200,000 years ago.

LUNAR LUNACY

HOW DID THE MOON FORM?

Our Moon may have formed when something crashed into the Earth 4.5 billion years ago—only about 100 million years after the Earth formed—sending a massive chunk of rock into space, where it stayed orbiting the planet.

WHAT COULD HAVE CRASHED INTO EARTH?

It may have been a small planet that smashed into Earth, knocking out a huge chunk that became the Moon. The planet has been called Theia.

WHAT IS THE MOON MADE OF?

The Earth and the Moon are made of exactly the same materials, so either the Moon is a chunk of the Earth or they both formed from the same stuff.

Our Moon is the largest moon belonging to a rocky planet. Mercury and Venus have no moons, and Mars' two moons are tiny in comparison with ours. There are only four larger moons in the whole solar system. Three belong to Jupiter and one to Saturn.

IS OUR MOON LARGE COMPARED TO EARTH?

The gas and ice giants have loads of moons, but they never add up to more than 0.1 percent of the mass of their planet. Our Moon, on its own, is 1.2 percent of the mass of Earth. Only the dwarf planet Pluto has a larger moon for its size, at nearly 12 percent of its mass.

DID YOU KNOW?

People once thought the Moon perfectly smooth; they didn't believe there could be anything imperfect in the heavens.

WHAT DOES THE MOON'S SURFACE LOOK LIKE?

The Moon's surface is pitted with craters from collisions with space rocks. Most were formed 3-4 billion years ago, but collisions are still happening. In 2013, a rock weighing 400 kg (880 lb) hurtled into the Moon, making a crater about 40 m (131 ft) across. The flash of the impact was visible from Earth.

DO THE MOON'S CRATERS HAVE NAMES?

Yes. Crater names include Robert, Gaston, and Isabel. The name "crater" was first used by Italian scientist Galileo in 1609. He took it from the Greek word for a cup for mixing water and wine.

WHAT DO THE MOON'S CRATERS LOOK LIKE?

Craters have a dip in the middle and a wall around the edge. The area outside the craters is scattered with smashed rock and beads of glass, made when molten rock cools. As there is no wind and rain to weather the craters, they remain unchanged for billions of years.

WHAT ARE THE AREAS OF LIGHT AND DARK WE SEE ON THE MOON?

The Moon has highlands and lowlands. The highlands are the light areas on the surface, and the low-lying areas are darker, made of rock rich in iron. The highland rock is much older than the darker, lowland rock.

ARE THERE SEAS ON THE MOON?

The astronomer Johannes Kepler named the low areas on the Moon "maria" (seas) in the 1600s, thinking there were really areas of land and sea. The maria were actually once flooded with lava that poured from volcanoes. It cooled and hardened to a flat surface. Some maria have been made by asteroids punching holes in the Moon's surface, allowing the lava inside to leak out.

ARE SITES ON THE MOON PROTECTED?

The sites of the Moon landings are "lunar heritage sites," similar to the "world heritage sites" that are protected special places on Earth. The Sea of Tranquility area, with its abandoned Moon junk, will be left as an eternal memorial to our earliest explorations of the Moon.

ARE THERE STILL HUMAN FOOTPRINTS ON THE LUNAR SURFACE?

The Moon has no weather, such as rain and wind, to wipe out the tracks, meaning human footprints on the Moon will still be there in millions of years, unless an asteroid or meteor crashing into just the right spot destroys or covers them.

HOW ARE OLD LANDING SITES ON THE MOON PRESERVED?

When new probes are sent to crash into the Moon, they are aimed well away from the early landing sites to avoid damaging them.

DOES THE MOON NEED DUSTING?

The Moon is extremely dusty. It's entirely covered by a layer of small stones and dust called "regolith." In some of the lowlands, the regolith is just 2 m (6 ft) thick, but on the highlands it can be as deep as 20 m (66 ft).

HOW IS REGOLITH MADE?

Regolith is rock that has been ground to dust or small stones by repeated collisions from asteroids and meteors. It's mixed with tiny blobs of glassy minerals formed when molten rocks cooled quickly.

DID YOU KNOW?

It's because the Moon has a loose, dusty layer that the Apollo missions left footprints and tracks on the Moon. If it was solid rock, there would be none.

WHY DID LUNA 2 CRASH ON THE MOON?

The Soviet craft Luna 2 was deliberately crashed into the Moon's surface on September 13, 1959. It was the first object from Earth ever to land on another celestial body. Luna 2 let out a cloud of gas as it neared the Moon that grew to 650 km (400 miles) wide to let scientists on Earth track its progress by telescope. An earlier Luna 1 mission missed the Moon, sailing straight past, and is still moving around the Sun.

WHEN DID WE FIRST SEE THE FAR SIDE OF THE MOON?

No one saw the far side of the Moon until 1959, when the Soviet spacecraft Luna 3 flew around the back and sent photos of it. The other, hidden, side of the Moon has a much thicker and older crust and many more craters than "our" side.

WHY DO WE ALWAYS SEE THE SAME SIDE OF THE MOON?

The Moon takes as long to turn once on its axis as it does to travel all the way around the Earth, so the same side of the Moon is always visible from Earth.

WHAT ARE MOON TREES?

Moon trees have grown from spacefaring seeds. Apollo 14 carried 500 tree seeds on a trip around the Moon (but they didn't land). The seeds were from Loblolly Pine, Sycamore, Sweetgum, Redwood, and Douglas Fir trees.

WHERE ARE THE MOON TREES GROWING?

Returned to Earth, nearly all the seeds grew into trees. Most Moon trees are in the USA, but there are also some in Japan, Brazil, and Switzerland. Second-generation Moon trees, grown from seeds or cuttings from the original Moon trees, are growing in the USA, England, Italy, and Switzerland.

HOW MUCH MOON ROCK IS ON EARTH?

Six Apollo Moon missions brought back 2,196 samples of Moon rock and dust. NASA's samples of Moon rock are kept at the Johnson Space Center in Houston, Texas, USA, and are sent out to scientists when they need them for research.

DID THE MOON HAVE A SISTER?

In 2011, some scientists suggested that Earth once had two moons. The second, smaller, moon would have been 1,270 km (790 miles) across—about one third the size of the surviving Moon.

WHAT HAPPENED TO IT?

It would have lasted about 70 million years before crashing into the present Moon. Instead of making a crater, the unlucky moon would have been smeared all over one side of the survivor. This could be why the far side of the Moon has a much thicker crust than the near side.

ARE THERE VOLCANOES ON THE MOON?

The Moon's large volcanoes have probably been dead for about a billion years, but some much smaller ones seem to have erupted more recently—perhaps as little as 18 million years ago. They might erupt again one day!

HOW CAN YOU LOSE WEIGHT ON THE MOON?

Gravity on the Moon is only about one sixth of Earth's gravity. That means that an astronaut who weighs 82 kg (180 lb) on Earth will weigh only 14 kg (30 lb) on the Moon.

HOW DOES LOWER GRAVITY AFFECT ASTRONAUTS?

Lower gravity means astronauts can leap and bounce in ways they never could on Earth. But they also fall over more—we need at least 15 percent of Earth's gravity to give our bodies a good idea of which way is up. Everything else weighs less, too, so astronauts can pick up objects that would be far too heavy for them to lift on Earth.

DOES THE MOON HAVE AN ATMOSPHERE?

The Moon's very thin atmosphere is made of helium, argon, possibly neon, ammonia, methane, and carbon dioxide. It's nothing like Earth's atmosphere, which has just 1 percent argon and tiny amounts of the others.

HOW DOES THE MOON'S ATMOSPHERE COMPARE TO EARTH'S?

If you collected a jug of Earth atmosphere and a jug of thin Moon atmosphere, the Earth jug would contain 10,000 billion times as many molecules (particles) as the Moon jug.

COULD WE BREATHE ON THE MOON?

We wouldn't be able to breathe on the Moon, even if the atmosphere was much thicker, as it doesn't have the same gases as Earth's atmosphere.

WHAT IS MOONLIGHT?

The surface of the Moon is actually dark, as it doesn't give off any natural light of its own. The bright light we see in the night's sky is light from the Sun reflecting off the surface of the Moon.

HOW LONG DO MOONQUAKES LAST?

Most earthquakes last just a few seconds, and even the longest are over in two minutes. But moonquakes can keep going for 10 minutes. If we ever build a space station on the Moon, it will have to be made of slightly flexible material so it isn't cracked by moonquakes.

DID YOU KNOW?

The Moon's orbit around Earth is not a perfect circle. At its closest (called "perigee"), the Moon is 356,500 km (221,500 miles) away. When it's farthest away (called "apogee"), it's 406,700 km (252,700 miles) from Earth.

HOW MANY PEOPLE HAVE SET FOOT ON THE MOON?

Only 12 people have ever set foot on the Moon. Six of the astronauts also drove rovers, or "moon buggies," over the surface. No one has landed on the Moon more than once. All 12 people were white, male Americans.

HOW FAST DOES THE MOON TRAVEL AROUND EARTH?

The Moon travels around Earth at 1 km per second (0.64 miles per second)—or 3,600 km/h (2,237 mph).

WHO WAS THE LAST PERSON TO LAND ON THE MOON?

The last visitor left the Moon on December 14, 1972. NASA's Apollo 17 was the last crewed mission to the Moon. All the astronauts who have landed on the Moon went over a period of just over three years.

WHAT HAPPENED TO THE FIRST FLAG PLACED ON THE MOON?

The astronauts of the first Moon landing in 1969, Neil Armstrong and Buzz Aldrin, planted a US flag on the surface of the Moon. As there is no wind on the Moon, it wouldn't flutter like it would on Earth and had to be wired so that it didn't just droop down its pole. But the blast from the departing spacecraft blew the flag down.

IS THE MOON MOVING AWAY?

The Moon moves about 3.8 cm (1.5 in) further away from the Earth every year.

WILL THE MOON EVER LEAVE EARTH'S ORBIT?

Probably not—it would take billions of years for the Moon to get far enough away to leave our orbit.

HOW LONG WOULD IT TAKE TO GET TO THE MOON IN A JUMBO JET OR CAR?

If you could, it would take 17 days to fly to the Moon by jumbo jet. It's 384,000 km (240,000 miles) from the Earth to the Moon, and a Boeing 747 travels at around 965 km/h (600 mph). If you could go by car at 80 km/h (50 mph), it would take 200 days—nearly seven months!

HOW LONG DID IT TAKE APOLLO ASTRONAUTS TO REACH THE MOON?

The Apollo spacecraft each took only 3-4 days to reach the Moon. A rocket going to the Moon doesn't follow a straight path. Instead, it goes part or all of the way around the Earth and the Moon.

ARE EARTH'S TIDES CAUSED BY THE MOON?

The Moon's gravity pulls the water of the Earth's oceans, making the tides. High tide is when the water is pulled further up the beach by the Moon's gravity.

HOW DO TIDES WORK?

As the Earth turns, the water on the side closest to the Moon is pulled toward the Moon. The water on the opposite side also "piles up." Each bit of coast has two high tides each day, once when that area is closest to the Moon and once when it's farthest away.

DID YOU KNOW?

Apollo 14 astronaut Alan Shepard smuggled a makeshift golf club and two golf balls to the Moon in 1971, hoping to make a record-breaking shot. His second shot was whacked more than 183 m (600 ft), helped by low gravity and no air. The golf balls are still on the Moon.

HOW LONG IS A MOON DAY?

A day is the time it takes a celestial body to turn on its own axis. Earth's day is 24 hours long. The Moon takes 29.5 days to turn once on its axis, so a Moon day is 29.5 Earth days long.

HOW LONG IS A MOON YEAR?

Earth goes around the Sun once in 365 days, which is a year. The Moon's "year" is the 27 days it takes to go around the Earth, which is shorter than its day.

HOW HOT DOES IT GET ON THE MOON?

Each half of the Moon faces the Sun for half of its long day. It has extreme temperatures, as it has a long time to heat up during the day and cool down at night. It can get as hot as 127°C (260°F) during the daytime and drop to -173°C (-279°F) at night.

IS THERE WATER ON THE MOON?

The Moon is bone dry, but only on the surface. Scientists examined tiny glass beads made of volcanic rock on the Moon and found small amounts of water locked into them. The volcanic rock is widespread on the Moon.

IS THERE ENOUGH TO DRINK?

Water trapped in rock on the Moon is not easy to spot, but it might go down to great depths. The Moon might contain enough locked-away water to make a shallow ocean 90 cm (3 ft) deep over the whole surface.

IS THERE ICE ON THE MOON?

There is ice in at least one deep crater at the Moon's south pole. Sunlight never reaches the bottom, and ice can lurk there without thawing for billions of years.

WHY DO PHOTOS FROM THE MOON SHOW A BLACK, STARLESS SKY?

Most photos taken from the Moon don't show stars because the astronauts landed in daytime. As each day lasts two weeks on the Moon, it was never night. The Sun was too bright for stars to show up.

WHAT IS STARGAZING LIKE ON THE MOON?

The Moon has far too little atmosphere to scatter sunlight, so the sky appears black, not blue, as on Earth. This means you can see far more stars than you could ever see from Earth. With no light pollution or atmosphere, the stars are crystal clear.

DID YOU KNOW?

There's a dead astronomer on the Moon—or part of one. After the US astronomer Eugene Shoemaker died, some of his ashes were packed on to the Lunar Prospector Lander, which was crashed into the Moon on July 31, 1999.

WILL WE BUILD A MOON BASE?

We might build a base on the Moon. It could be used as a jumping-off point for other space trips, or a research station. A Moon base would need to be well insulated and heated or cooled because of the Moon's extreme hot and cold temperatures. It would have to be completely sealed to keep the air in, and able to recycle air. There is no liquid water, but colonists might be able to extract water that is locked inside rocks or frozen into ice.

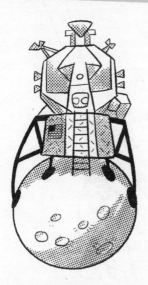

IS THE MOON SHRINKING?

Yes! When the Moon first formed, it was scalding hot. As it cooled, it shrank (because hot material takes up more space than the same material when it's cold). Cracks and ridges in the Moon's surface suggest that it's been shrinking in the last billion years. The Moon has probably shrunk by about 183 m (600 ft) across its width.

HOW BIG IS THE MOON'S BIGGEST CRATER?

The Aitken basin, near the Moon's south pole, is 2,500 km (1,550 miles) across. The lowest point of the basin's floor to the highest point of the surrounding wall is more than 13 km (8.1 miles). That's twice as high as Mount Everest!

WHAT CAUSED THE AITKEN BASIN?

It was made by an asteroid smashing into the Moon about 3.9 billion years ago. It gouged a hole in the Moon's surface, and pushed up walls of rock around the hole.

WHY DOES THE MOON COME OUT IN THE DAYTIME?

The Moon is above the horizon for roughly 12 hours a day, rising and setting once a day, so it's often visible in the daytime. It often either rises before sunset or sets after sunrise, so it overlaps with daylight and is not always out all night.

IS THERE A PICTURE ON THE MOON?

People have always seen pictures in the patterns on the full Moon, but they haven't all seen the same thing. Some have seen a person with a bundle of sticks, an old man with a lantern, or a woman with a fancy hairstyle and jewels. In China, Japan, and Korea, people see a rabbit making something in a pot—maybe medicine or rice cakes. Other cultures have seen a buffalo, moose, frog, toad, or dragon.

WHO OWNS THE MOON?

Some companies claim to sell areas of land on the Moon, and take people's money for it, but they have no rights to any of the Moon and the "ownership" is not recognized. In 1967, the International Outer Space Treaty declared that no one can own any part of outer space, including the Moon.

HAS ANYONE EVER CLAIMED IT?

One man from Germany claims the Moon was given to his family in 1756 by the King of Prussia, Frederick the Great.

WHAT HAVE WE LEFT BEHIND ON THE MOON?

For 4.5 billion years, the Moon was a garbage-free zone, then people started going there. Now there's around 187,400 kg (413,100 lb) of clutter there. We've left more than 70 vehicles on the Moon, including crashed spacecraft, used rovers, and discarded modules of spacecraft. Tools including hammers, rakes, shovels, and expensive cameras were all left behind by astronauts.

IS THERE ANYTHING GROSS LEFT ON THE MOON?

Some of the stuff left behind is really not very nice—used wet wipes, empty space-food packages, and 96 bags of human waste and vomit!

IS THERE A PLAQUE ON THE MOON?

There is a commemorative plaque attached to a leg of the abandoned Apollo 11 lander that bears the words: "Here men from the planet Earth first set foot upon the Moon, July 1969 AD. We came in peace for all mankind."

DID ASTRONAUTS LEAVE ANY SPECIAL MEMENTOS?

Apollo 11 astronauts left a satchel holding medals commemorating two Soviet cosmonauts, who died in 1967 and 1968, Vladimir Komarov and Yuri Gagarin. Another commemorative object is a patch from the Apollo 1 mission, which burst into flames before its launch, killing three astronauts.

PECULIAR PLANETS

HOW WAS THE SOLAR SYSTEM FORMED?

The solar system formed 4.5 billion years ago from a huge, whirling cloud of dust and gas. Pieces of matter started to clump together and, the heavier the lumps got, the more matter they attracted. The biggest lumps eventually became the Sun, the planets, and their moons.

WHY ARE SOME PLANETS ROCKY AND SOME GASSY?

The solar system has four rocky planets (Mercury, Venus, Earth, and Mars) which are nearest the Sun, and four planets made of gas (Saturn, Jupiter, Uranus and Neptune). When the solar system first formed, it was too hot near the Sun for gases to condense (squeeze together), so they were carried farther out to a colder region. Rock solidifies at much higher temperatures.

HOW BIG IS MERCURY?

Mercury, the nearest planet to the Sun, is barely bigger than our Moon, at just 4,878 km (3,030 miles) across. And it's shrinking! New cracks over the surface appear as the heat inside cools and shrinks.

HOW CLOSE IS MERCURY TO THE SUN?

Mercury is about 58 million km (36 million miles) from the Sun, just over a third as far away as Earth.

HOW LONG IS A DAY ON MERCURY?

The time taken by Mercury to turn on its axis is just under 59 Earth days long.

COULD MERCURY SPIN OUT OF ORBIT?

Some astronomers think that Jupiter's strong gravity is disrupting the orbit of Mercury. Mercury already has an odd orbit, and it's vulnerable to being knocked around.

COULD MERCURY CRASH INTO EARTH?

There are four possible outcomes, and none look good for Mercury! Mercury may crash into the Sun, be thrown out of the solar system entirely, crash into Venus, or crash into Earth. But don't worry—it's not due to happen for another 5-7 billion years.

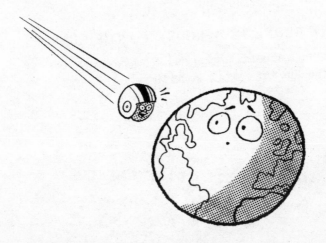

IS VENUS' DAY LONGER THAN ITS YEAR?

Venus, the second planet from the Sun, takes 225 Earth days to orbit around it. It turns on its own axis so slowly that it takes 243 Earth days to make one full rotation.

DOES VENUS SPIN THE "WRONG" WAY AROUND?

Venus and Uranus both rotate the opposite way from all the other planets. This may be because they were both knocked over by an early collision with a large asteroid.

IS VENUS WORTH A VISIT?

Venus is the hottest planet in the solar system, with a surface temperature of up to 462°C (864°F), because its atmosphere traps heat close to the planet. On Venus, you would be crushed under atmospheric pressure 93 times that on Earth—and burned by the acidic clouds.

WHO OWNS MARS?

In 1997, three men from Yemen sued NASA for "invading" Mars. They say that their families inherited the planet from ancestors who lived 3,000 years ago. They based their claim on myths from early civilizations in ancient Saudi Arabia. NASA did not agree that the men own Mars, and they plan to continue exploring.

IS THERE A MARTIAN IN RUSSIA?

Russian boy Boriska Kipriyanovich says he was once a Martian and has been reborn on Earth. From early childhood, he has told his parents about life on Mars, where he says the Martians live underground.

ARE THERE CANALS ON MARS?

In 1877, Italian astronomer Giovanni Schiaparelli drew the first map of Mars. He was convinced he could see straight lines crisscrossing the surface of Mars. He called them "canali," which means "channels," but people who didn't speak Italian thought that meant canals. By 1909, astronomers with better telescopes showed there were no canals.

WHY IS MARS RED?

Mars is rusty. It's known as the red planet, and its surface has red rocks and soil because there's a lot of iron oxide rust in them.

IS MARS BIGGER THAN EARTH?

Mars is much smaller than Earth—it's 6,779 km (4,212 miles) across, or just over half the width of Earth. Mars would fit inside Earth six times.

DOES MARS HAVE ANY MOONS?

Mars has two moons, but they're tiny. Phobos is 22.5 km (13.8 miles) across and Demos is just 12.4 km (7.8 miles) across. Both look a little like potatoes—they aren't large enough to have spun themselves into spheres.

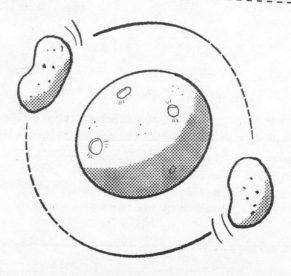

WHERE IS THE LARGEST VOLCANO IN THE SOLAR SYSTEM?

Mars has a volcano the size of France. Olympus Mons is 25 km (16 miles) tall, while the highest mountain on Earth, Mount Everest, is just over a third of that size at 8.8 km (5.5 miles) high. Olympus Mons is not only tall—it's 100 times the volume of the largest volcano on Earth.

IS OLYMPUS MONS DANGEROUS?

Olympus Mons has not erupted for around 25 million years and appears to be extinct.

DID JUPITER DESTROY A PLANET?

Jupiter may have destroyed a dwarf planet. Its remains orbit the Sun between Mars and Jupiter as billions or even trillions of chunks of rock called the Asteroid Belt. If another planet tried to form here, massive Jupiter would have disrupted it, scattering the clumps so that they collided and broke up.

HOW BIG IS THE ASTEROID BELT?

Some of the asteroids are big enough to qualify as dwarf planets themselves. Most of the Asteroid Belt is empty space. If you could stand on one asteroid, you'd struggle to see the next nearest.

WHICH PLANET HAS THE SHORTEST DAY?

The shortest day in the solar system is on Jupiter. There, a day is just under 10 hours long, and a year is nearly 12 Earth years long. That means there are more than 10,000 Jupiter days in a Jupiter year.

DO ALL THE PLANETS HAVE MOONS?

Earth isn't the only planet with a Moon. Mercury and Venus don't have any, but Jupiter, Saturn, Uranus, and Neptune all have lots.

HOW MANY MOONS DO JUPITER AND SATURN HAVE?

Saturn has at least 61 and Jupiter at least 79. Because the planets are so large, their gravity reaches far into space, letting them capture passing lumps of rock and ice and dragging them into orbit as moons.

COULD YOU STAND ON JUPITER?

You couldn't stand up on Jupiter as there's no solid surface. Instead, you would sink through 60,000 km (37,000 miles) of gas and thick soupy gloop before perhaps reaching a solid core.

COULD JUPITER BECOME A STAR?

Jupiter is made mostly of hydrogen, just like the Sun, but to work as a star, it would need to be much bigger. Stars produce heat and light through a process called nuclear fusion, but Jupiter is too small to do that. We would have to find another 79 planets just like Jupiter and smash them all together to make a new star.

WHERE IS THE SMELLIEST PLACE IN THE SOLAR SYSTEM?

Jupiter's moon Io is the most volcanic place in the solar system. It has 400 active volcanoes, some of them shooting smelly fumes of sulfur 500 km (310 miles) out into space.

WHICH PLANET HAS THE STRONGEST GRAVITY?

The more mass an object has, the more gravitational pull it has. Jupiter is the most massive planet in the solar system and has the strongest gravitational force.

HOW HEAVY WOULD YOU FEEL ON JUPITER?

If you could visit Jupiter, you would weigh two-and-a-half times as much as you weigh on Earth.

WHAT'S THE WEATHER LIKE ON JUPITER?

Jupiter's Great Red Spot is a storm twice as wide as the Earth. Winds there blow at 644 km/h (400 mph), with storms sometimes lasting for hundreds of years.

WHAT IS THE SOLAR SYSTEM'S BIGGEST MOON?

The largest moon in the solar system is Ganymede, which belongs to Jupiter. It has a thin atmosphere of oxygen and a salty ocean 200 km (124 miles) below the surface.

WHERE CAN YOU GO SKATING NEAR SATURN?

The surface of Saturn's moon Enceladus is 99 percent water (or, rather, ice). It has ice volcanoes that shoot 250 kg (550 lb) of water into space every second.

IS TRITON A GOOD PLACE TO GO ON VACATION?

Not unless you like it cold! Triton, a moon of Neptune, is one of the coldest places in the solar system. The temperature drops to a bone-chilling –235°C (–391°F). Not happy with just being super-chilly, Triton is a bit of an oddball because it rotates the opposite way to Neptune. Most moons rotate in the same direction as their planets.

WHAT ARE SATURN'S RINGS MADE OF?

Saturn's rings are made of billions of particles of rock, dust, and ice. These might be solid chunks of rock, or perhaps something like dirty snowballs, with smaller lumps frozen together. Some might be the size of a bus, but many are too small to see.

HOW BIG ARE SATURN'S RINGS?

Some of Saturn's rings are only 10 m (33 ft) thick, but they are 400,000 km (240,000 miles) across—farther than the distance from Earth to the Moon. There are 500-1,000 separate rings, with big and small gaps between them.

COULD SATURN FLOAT?

Although its rings are rocky, the planet Saturn is light and gassy. It could even float in water—if you could find a bathtub big enough!

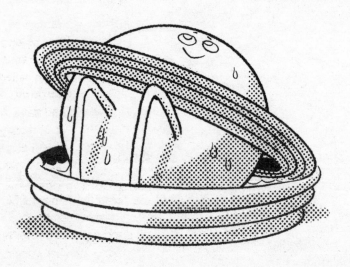

IS URANUS THE WRONG WAY UP?

Uranus is the only planet in the solar system that lies on its side. It might have been knocked sideways by a collision with something billions of years ago.

WHO DISCOVERED URANUS?

The first planet discovered since the Stone Age was Uranus. A German-English amateur astronomer called William Herschel spotted it in 1781.

WAS URANUS NEARLY CALLED GEORGE?

Herschel wanted to name it after the king of England, so Uranus could have been called George. George was pleased and gave Herschel a lot of money. He used it to build bigger and better telescopes. Herschel became a full-time astronomer who made other important discoveries, but he never found another planet.

HOW LONG IS A YEAR ON URANUS?

Uranus takes 84 Earth years to orbit the Sun. That means that each pole gets 42 years of daylight and 42 years of darkness!

COULD NEPTUNE AND URANUS BE SET ON FIRE?

A gas called methane makes Neptune and Uranus look blue. Methane ice is also flammable, so if there were oxygen on these planets, the ice giants could burn.

WHY ARE NEPTUNE AND URANUS SLUDGY?

Neptune and Uranus are ice planets, but that doesn't mean they're just big chunks of ice. Below the atmosphere is a thick layer of water, methane, and ammonia, which probably form sludgy ice. Right in the middle, there is likely a small core of rock and ice.

WAS NEPTUNE ONLY DISCOVERED A YEAR AGO?

Yes, if you think in Neptune years. Neptune was first seen in 1846, which is more than 170 Earth years ago. But Neptune is so far from the Sun that it takes about 165 Earth years to go around it once, so it has only completed one circuit (one year) since it was first discovered.

HOW MANY DAYS ARE IN A NEPTUNE YEAR?

Neptune spins quite quickly on its axis, so its day is just 16 hours and 6 minutes long. That means it has more than 60,190 days in its year. That's a long time between birthdays!

WHERE CAN I GO FOR A LONG SUMMER VACATION?

If you lived on Neptune, you might spend your entire life in its 80-year summer—but you could be unlucky and spend your whole life in winter.

WHERE IS THE SOLAR SYSTEM'S WINDIEST SPOT?

The stormiest storm in the solar system is on Neptune. Its Great Dark Spot, seen in 1979, had winds of 2,400 km/h (1,500 mph). Outside the Spot, winds regularly tear around the planet at nearly 600 m per second (2,000 ft per second).

DOES IT RAIN DIAMONDS ON NEPTUNE?

Storms on Neptune and Uranus might produce diamond "hail" from carbon under huge pressure. The diamond rain could have produced lakes or even oceans of liquid diamond, maybe with floating diamond icebergs.

WHO DISCOVERED PLUTO?

Businessman Percival Lowell built the Lowell Observatory in Arizona, USA, in 1896 to explore the "canals" reported on Mars. When they turned out not to exist, he started looking for a new planet. He photographed Pluto in 1915, but as it was much fainter than he expected, he didn't recognize it. Pluto was officially discovered by Clyde Tombaugh at Lowell's observatory fifteen years later, in 1930.

HOW MUCH WOULD YOU WEIGH ON PLUTO?

On Pluto, you would weigh just one fifteenth of your weight on Earth.

IS IT COMPLETELY DARK ON PLUTO?

Pluto is up to 7.5 billion km (4.67 billion miles) away, so it gets a lot less sunlight than Earth. But it's not completely dark—there's as much light at midday on Pluto as there is on Earth just after sunset.

IS PLUTO WET?

If you could collect all the water from Earth and make it into a ball, it would be 692 km (430 miles) across. If you did the same to Pluto, it would make a ball 1,368 km (850 miles) across.

COULD THERE BE FISH IN PLUTO'S WATER?

Pluto's huge ocean stretches all around the planet under a thick crust of ice. But it's a poisonous chemical mix that won't be full of Plutonic sea creatures.

WHY DO COMETS HAVE TAILS?

If you see a comet in the sky, it looks spectacular—a bright, shining speck with a long glowing tail. But close up, comets are messy lumps of rock and dust. As they get close to the Sun, ice evaporates and the freed gas and dust make up their tail. The tails always face away from the Sun.

HOW OFTEN DO WE SEE COMETS?

Nearby comets drop by every 200 years or so. They orbit the Sun in a giant ellipse (squashed circle), and we see them when they come close to the Earth. Comets spend most of their time in an area called the Kuiper Belt, beyond the orbit of Neptune. There are trillions of big and small comets there.

HOW BIG IS THE LARGEST KNOWN COMET?

The largest known comet, McNaught, is 25 km (15 miles) wide.

WHEN WAS HALLEY'S COMET FIRST SPOTTED?

Halley's comet has been recorded for more than 2,200 years.

WHY WERE PEOPLE FRIGHTENED OF HALLEY'S COMET?

When Halley's comet was due to be seen in 1910, people panicked and thought it would be the end of the world. Scammers even sold comet-proof hats to stop radiation, and pills to protect people from comet "poison."

DID HALLEY'S COMET BRING DISASTER?

In the past, all kinds of disasters were blamed on innocent comets, but they never destroyed the world. But 1910 was the first time scientists could work out that Earth would pass through the comet's tail. People feared it would be poisonous and possibly wipe out life on Earth. But we're all still here...

HOW LONG IS THE TAIL ON HALLEY'S COMET?

Halley's comet has a tail that can be up to 100 million km (60 million miles) long.

HOW LONG WILL HALLEY'S COMET LAST?

Each journey by the Sun melts some of the comet, so eventually it will be all gone. Halley's comet loses a layer 10 m (33 feet) thick on each visit, so will last another 76,000 years.

WHEN CAN I SEE HALLEY'S COMET FROM EARTH?

Halley's comet is seen every 76 years. It is due to pass close enough to Earth again in 2061.

WHERE IS THE BEST PLACE TO LOOK FOR LIFE IN SPACE?

Jupiter's moon Europa and Saturn's moon Enceladus are probably the best places to look for life in the solar system beyond Earth. Enceladus has a layer of ice 5 km (3 miles) thick over an ocean 65 km (40 miles) deep. Warm water below the surface could be home to microbes, as it is on Earth.

WAS THERE REALLY A PLANET NAMED EASTER BUNNY?

There was a dwarf planet named Easter Bunny, but only until it got its permanent name, Makemake. It was given the name because it was found just after Easter in 2005. Makemake was the god of fertility in the myths of the Rapa Nui people of Easter Island.

WHERE IS MAKEMAKE?

Discovered in 2005, this little world is 45 times as far from the Sun as Earth is. It's cold and dark and tiny, at just 1,450 km (900 miles) across, and has at least one small moon. Makemake takes 309 Earth years to go around the Sun.

ARE WE LEAVING THE SUN?

The planets are slowly moving away from the Sun at a rate of about 15 cm (6 in) a year. Scientists aren't sure why. One reason might be that, as the Sun gradually uses itself up making heat and light energy, its mass reduces. It then has less gravitational "pull" to hold on to the planets.

IS THE SUN SLOWING DOWN?

The Sun slows down as it spins, which might reduce its ability to keep the planets nearby. The planets themselves slow it down—their gravitational pull has a braking effect on it. Earth reduces the Sun's speed by three milliseconds each century (0.00003 seconds per year).

DID YOU KNOW?

One way that you can tell stars and planets apart without a telescope is by watching for twinkling. Stars twinkle, but planets don't. Stars create their own light; planets just reflect the light of the Sun (our star).

IS THERE ANOTHER PLANET BEYOND PLUTO?

It's possible that there is another planet beyond Neptune and even Pluto. Planet Nine, NASA suggests, could be 20 times farther from the Sun than Neptune.

WHAT COULD PLANET NINE BE LIKE?

The extra planet is likely to be an icy gas planet like Neptune and Uranus, ten times the mass of Earth. That's big but much less massive than the gas giants. It could take Planet Nine 10,000-20,000 Earth years to orbit the Sun just once.

WHY DO SCIENTISTS THINK THERE IS A PLANET NINE?

The gravity of Planet Nine—if it's there—would explain the odd activity of some objects in the Kuiper Belt. Some have a very tilted orbit, move at an angle to the rest of the solar system, or orbit the Sun in the wrong direction.

THE OUTER LIMITS

DO WE NEED THE SUN?

The Sun provides all the energy that life on Earth needs. Its gravity keeps Earth and the other planets of the solar system in orbit. We couldn't live without it!

IS OUR SUN FIT AND HEALTHY?

Our Sun is a common type of star—it's a medium size, yellow dwarf main sequence star, 4.6 billion years old. That means it's at a healthy stage in the middle of its working life, pumping out energy as heat and light.

WHY IS THE SUN EIGHT MINUTES LATE?

It takes eight minutes for light to reach us from the Sun. Light moves very, very quickly—it covers nearly 400,000 km (248,500 miles) every second. But the Sun is so far away that it still takes eight minutes and 20 seconds for its light to get to us.

HOW HEAVY IS THE SUN?

The Sun weighs 330,000 times as much as Earth. It contains 99.8 percent of the mass of the solar system. All the planets, moons, comets, and asteroids make up the rest.

HOW HOT IS THE SUN?

The temperature at the Sun's surface is 6,000°C (11,000°F). Right in the middle, where all the action is, the temperature is 15 million°C (27 million°F). The atmosphere around the edge of the Sun is called the corona. It's much hotter than the surface, at 1-10 million°C (1.7-17 million°F). No one knows why.

HOW MANY EARTHS COULD YOU SQUEEZE INTO THE SUN?

Earth would fit inside the Sun 1.3 million times over.

IS THE SUN SHRINKING?

The Sun gets slimmer by the mass of the Earth every 47 million years. It sounds like a lot, but not for the Sun. Its current mass is 2,000,000,000,000,000,000,000,000,000,000 kg (2,200,000,000,000,000,000,000,000,000 tons). By the end of its life, in around 5 billion years, it will have lost only 0.034 percent of its current mass.

WHAT WILL HAPPEN WHEN THE SUN "DIES?"

When the Sun runs out of hydrogen, it will swell to a red giant, taking in Mercury and Venus. Then it will lose its outer layers, leaving a hard, dense white dwarf about the size of the Earth—but still with much of its mass. Gravity at the surface will be 100,000 times Earth's gravity, and it will be 20 times as hot as the Sun's outer parts are now. Heat escapes slowly into space, so it will take trillions of years to turn into a cold, dead black dwarf.

IS OUR SUN QUITE A SMALL STAR?

Nearly every star you can see is bigger than the Sun. Stars come in lots of sizes, but they're a long way away. From Earth, you can only see the biggest and brightest stars. The Sun is the fourth smallest star we can see from Earth without a telescope or binoculars. The other three are very faint.

IS THE POLE STAR BRIGHTER THAN OUR SUN?

The Pole Star, Polaris, is a bright star in the night sky. It's 2,200 times as bright as the Sun, but so far away it looks like a pinprick.

ARE RED STARS THE HOTTEST?

Red-hot stars are actually the coolest. We're used to thinking of red things as super hot, but that's only because we link fire and heat with red. Red is the first type of light to shine out as something gets hot, so it comes from the coolest hot things. The hottest stars shine with pale blue light.

WHERE IS THE NEXT-NEAREST STAR?

After the Sun, the next-nearest star is called Proxima Centauri. It's nearly 40 trillion km (25 trillion miles) away.

WHAT IS A LIGHT YEAR?

The time light can travel in an entire year is called a light year. It's nearly 9.5 trillion km (6 trillion miles). That's 9,500,000,000,000 km (6,000,000,000,000 miles). Astronomers measure distances in space in light years.

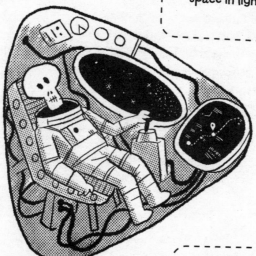

HOW LONG WOULD IT TAKE TO GET TO PROXIMA CENTAURI?

Even in the fastest spacecraft we have, it would take 76,000 years to get Proxima Centauri.

CAN I SEE PROXIMA CENTAURI IN THE NIGHT SKY?

Proxima Centauri is not very bright, so we can't see it at all without a telescope.

HOW BIG ARE THE LARGEST STARS?

The biggest stars of all are supergiants. Their mass can be 100 times the mass of the Sun, and they are hundreds of times as wide. Supergiants produce energy at an astonishing rate. They can produce 100,000 times as much energy as the Sun, so they shine 100,000 times brighter. Even though they are big, they whizz through their fuel supply quickly. They last only a few million years before they use up all of their fuel.

WHICH STAR IS THE BIGGEST?

It's hard to say exactly which star is the largest. One contender for the title is NML Cygni, 5,300 light years away. It could be anywhere between 1,642 and 2,775 times as wide as the Sun.

WHICH STAR IS THE BRIGHTEST?

The brightest star is called Pistol. It shines up to 10 million times as brightly as the Sun. So much radiation comes from it that even if it has any planets they could not support life.

WHAT ARE SUNSPOTS?

Sunspots are dark patches on the surface of the Sun. They're not really dark—they just look dark by comparison with the super-bright areas around them. Sunspots are cooler than the rest of the Sun's surface, but they're still pretty hot, at 4,200°C (7,600°F).

HOW BIG ARE SUNSPOTS?

They're not small spots—they can be 160,000 km (100,000 miles) across. That's 12 times as wide as the Earth.

WHAT IS A SUPERNOVA?

Stars more than eight times the mass of the Sun eventually explode in a spectacular supernova. The explosion lasts a week or more, shining more brightly than any star in the sky. The last supernova seen clearly from Earth happened in 1604.

ARE ALL THE STARS IN THE SKY IN OUR GALAXY?

All the stars you can see at night are in our galaxy, the Milky Way. The Milky Way is so vast, and the stars in it so bright, that we can't see the stars outside it.

CAN WE CAN SEE ANY OTHER GALAXIES IN THE NIGHT SKY?

Not everything you can see in the night sky is in the Milky Way. The "star" below Orion's belt and one of the "stars" of Andromeda are both nebulae. They are not single stars but entire galaxies outside the Milky Way. When you look at these, the fuzzy cloud of light you see is collected from hundreds of billions of stars.

HOW MANY STARS ARE IN THE MILKY WAY?

There are up to 400 billion stars in the Milky Way.

HOW BIG IS THE MILKY WAY?

The Milky Way is a disk 100,000 light years across—but only 1,000 light years thick. It's a spiral galaxy, with "arms" trailing out into space. We are on a smaller arm, 28,000 light years from the middle.

WHERE IS THE MILKY WAY IN SPACE?

The Milky Way is part of a group of galaxies called, unimaginatively, the Local Group. Between one billion and one trillion years from now, the Milky Way and all the other galaxies of the Local Group will have merged into a single mega galaxy.

HOW FAST IS THE SUN MOVING AROUND THE MILKY WAY?

The Sun goes around the middle of the Milky Way at 828,000 km/h (514,000 mph)—one circuit takes 230–240 million years.

WHAT'S IN THE MIDDLE OF THE MILKY WAY?

There is probably a supermassive black hole at the middle of the Milky Way. It has the mass of four million Suns and is called Sagittarius A* (pronounced "A-star"). All galaxies probably have a huge black hole in the middle, with the mass of millions or billions of stars crushed into a small space. As they take in more dust, gas, and other matter, they grow even larger.

WHAT IS A BLACK HOLE?

Black holes aren't holes at all. It's an area where matter is so squashed there is no space in it at all, not even within the atoms. Anything that gets too close to a black hole is pulled toward it and squashed along with everything else. That's how black holes grow.

HOW MANY BLACK HOLES ARE IN OUR GALAXY?

There are more than 100 million black holes in the Milky Way.

CAN YOU SEE A BLACK HOLE?

It's impossible to see a black hole in black space—it looks like nothing. Although we can't see black holes with telescopes, there are giveaway signs that they are there. Where stars or other objects seem to go around an empty patch of sky, there might be a black hole lurking there.

WHAT HAPPENS IF YOU GET SUCKED INTO A BLACK HOLE?

Most astronomers think matter that gets pulled into a black hole is compressed and destroyed. But a few think black holes are tunnels to another universe. At the end of the tunnel—or wormhole—the matter is spat out of a white hole where it's used to make—well, whatever that universe has in it.

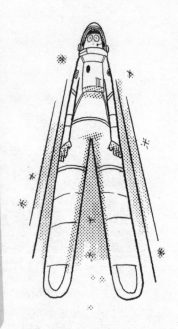

WHAT IS THE NEAREST GALAXY TO OUR OWN?

Andromeda is the closest galaxy, 2.5 million light years away.

IS OUR GALAXY GOING TO CRASH INTO ANOTHER?

Yes. The Milky Way and the galaxy closest to it, the Andromeda Galaxy, are heading for a crash. Andromeda is moving toward us at 110 km (68 miles) per second; the collision is due in about 4 billion years. There's lots of space between stars, so it will probably be a largely peaceful merger with very few stars actually colliding.

COULD IT BE A THREE-WAY CRASH?

The Triangulum, the third largest galaxy in our Local Group, is moving in the same direction. The new, combined galaxy has already been named: Milkdromeda or Milkomeda.

HOW DID THE UNIVERSE BEGIN?

The start of the universe is called the Big Bang, but it was silent—there was no "bang." There was no explosion to see either—even if there had been anything with eyes to see it.

WHAT HAPPENED AT THE BIG BANG?

All space, time, matter, and energy in the universe were created in an instant. Everything expanded from a tiny point to the size of a grapefruit in just 0.000 00000000000000000 00000000001 seconds. In this time, the universe doubled in size 90 times.

WHAT WERE THE FIRST THINGS TO APPEAR IN THE UNIVERSE?

The first pieces of matter—nuclei, the middles of atoms—appeared in the first minutes. This was almost all hydrogen and helium.

WHAT HAPPENED BEFORE THE BIG BANG?

No one knows what, if anything, existed before the Big Bang. "Before" might be meaningless.

IS THE UNIVERSE GETTING BIGGER AND FASTER?

The Big Bang was the sudden appearance of everywhere (all space-time), but then "everywhere" got bigger. It didn't expand into empty space, but space appeared in between the stuff of the universe, pushing it apart. Around 5-6 billion years after the Big Bang, the speed at which the universe was growing bigger increased. So it got bigger more quickly, and it is still getting bigger, faster and faster.

WILL THE UNIVERSE GET BIGGER FOREVER?

The universe could keep getting bigger quickly until it's just a thin, dark soup of matter where nothing can hold itself together—a Big Rip. Or it could reach a final size where matter is so far apart that there is no movement or heat. Or everything could bounce back toward the middle in a reverse of the Big Bang—a Big Crunch. It's not something to worry about; whatever happens could be anywhere from 2.8 billion years away to never.

HOW DO WE KNOW THE POLE STAR IS STILL BURNING?

We don't! Polaris is 323 light years away, so we see it as it was 323 years ago. If it had exploded in 1900, we wouldn't see the explosion until around 200 years from now.

WHY WILL IT TAKE SO LONG?

Light takes a very, very long time to reach us from distant objects in the sky. If any aliens 67 million light years away looked at Earth with a super-powerful telescope, they would see dinosaurs roaming the planet—they would see 67 million years into the past!

DID YOU KNOW?

A teaspoonful of neutron star would weigh tens of millions of tons.

HAVE WE TRIED TO CONTACT ALIENS?

In 1974, astronomers in Puerto Rico beamed a radio message toward a group of stars huddled at the edge of the Milky Way. This cosmic "hello" thrown out into the universe carried a set of simple pictures intended to tell aliens we exist. It was the most powerful radio signal ever transmitted.

WHEN MIGHT WE GET AN ANSWER?

The bunch of 300,000 stars is called M13. It's 21,000 light years away, so even if anyone picks it up, we won't get an answer for 42,000 years.

HAS THE SOLAR SYSTEM HAD ANY VISITORS FROM BEYOND?

Late in 2017, an asteroid from another star system in the Milky Way whizzed into our solar system, looped round the Sun, and left again. The splinter of rock was named Oumuamua, from the Hawaiian word for "scout" or "messenger."

HOW COLD IS DEEP SPACE?

The temperature in deep space is about -270.5°C (-455°F). That's only a few degrees warmer than the coldest temperature that is possible anywhere, -273.15°C (-459.7°F). At that point, all the particles in matter stop moving—nothing can be colder.

IS ALL SPACE FREEZING COLD?

Not all space is freezing. Gas between stars, or the solar wind (stream of particles) from stars, can be very hot, reaching thousands or even millions of degrees.

HOW BIG IS THE UNIVERSE?

The universe is at least 93 billion light years across. The edge of the visible universe is 46.5 billion light years away. That should mean the light left it 46.5 billion years ago, but that's not possible as the universe is only 13.8 billion years old.

IS THERE MORE THAN ONE UNIVERSE?

Some scientists suspect we're part of a multiverse—an infinite number of universes that branch off all the time. This means all possibilities become real. There's a universe where you had toast for breakfast and one where you didn't.

WHAT'S BIGGER THAN A LIGHT YEAR?

The biggest unit astronomers can use is the gigaparsec—which is a billion parsecs. A parsec is 3.262 light years, or about 31 trillion km (19 trillion miles). Earth is 14 gigaparsecs from the edge of the observable universe.

HOW MANY STARS ARE THERE IN OUR GALAXY?

Our galaxy probably has around 400 billion stars.

HOW MANY GALAXIES ARE THERE IN THE UNIVERSE?

There are probably between 100 billion and a trillion galaxies. If they were all a similar size, there would be at least 400 billion x 100 billion stars, which is 20 sextillion (20,000,000,000,000,000,000,000) stars.

ARE THERE MORE STARS IN THE UNIVERSE THAN GRAINS OF SAND ON EARTH?

Researchers in Hawaii worked out the area and depth of all the world's beaches and the volume of a grain of sand. Then they calculated that there are 7.5 quintillion (7,500,000,000,000,000,000) grains of sand on Earth. So there are more than 2,500 times as many stars as there are grains of sand.

WHAT IS THE UNIVERSE MADE OF?

We don't know what most of the universe is. Adding up all the bits we know about, we can account for only one twentieth of the total mass of the universe. Ninety-five percent is unknown.

WHAT IS DARK ENERGY?

The 99 percent unknown mass of the universe is made of dark energy (68 percent) and dark matter (27 percent). No one really knows what they are. Dark matter could be lots of brown dwarfs or patches of dense matter that don't emit light. Or it could be a type of matter we have never met.

WHAT DOES DARK ENERGY DO?

Empty space is also full of dark energy. It springs from nowhere, pushing matter farther and farther apart and making the universe larger from within. But no one understands it or knows exactly how it works.

HOW CAN WE CONTACT ALIENS?

The Search for Extra Terrestrial Intelligence (SETI) uses radio telescopes to look for evidence of aliens. It will only find aliens advanced enough to send out radio signals. Radio signals are our best hope of finding intelligent aliens, as we can't see conditions on distant planets.

WHY HAVEN'T WE HEARD FROM ALIENS?

Astronomers have a few ideas why: We might be too early—the first civilization to develop radio and space travel. Maybe they're waiting for us to get more advanced before they get in touch. Perhaps we just haven't looked long enough to find them. Or, maybe we're too late—other civilizations have come and gone.

MIGHT ALIENS BE AVOIDING US?

Maybe! They could have learned that contact with Earth is dangerous, so they're staying quiet or hiding.